How to Format Your Book, for Publishing

How To For You
MercerPublications.com

How to For Your Series #11

Dorothy May Mercer

Dorothy May Mercer

ISBN 13: 978-1-62329-089-4

ISBN 10: 1-62329-089-9

©2019 Mercer Publications & Ministries, Inc., Publisher

Stanwood, Michigan &SA 49346

All rights reserved.

How to Format Your Book, for Publishing

TABLE OF CONTENTS

INTRODUCTION 7

CHAPTER 1 DESIGNING PAGES AND TYPE 9
Paragraphs	9
Page Layout	9
Margins	10
Line Spacing	10
Typeface	11

CHAPTER 2 STYLE YOUR CHAPTER HEADINGS. 13

CHAPTER 3 ORDER OF OPENING PAGES 15
The Reverse Arrows	16
Common Mistakes:	17

CHAPTER 4 PICTURES 19
Moving Your Picture	21

CHAPTER 5 WRITING YOUR BOOK 23
Designing Chapters	23
Styling Non Fiction	23
Styling Fiction	24
Alignment	27

CHAPTER 6 AFTER "THE END" 29
Non Fiction   **29**
   Footnotes 29
   Reference Pages 30
Fiction: **30**

CHAPTER 7 FINAL FORMATTING OF PRINT BOOK 33
Creating Sections   **33**
Creating Headers   **34**
   Designing Your Headers 36
Installing Page Numbers   **37**
Remove All Color   **39**
   Save a PDF Version 40

CHAPTER 8 FORMAT YOUR EBOOK 41
Ads and Links   **41**

Dorothy May Mercer

How to Format Your Book, for Publishing

Introduction

When I write a book for publishing, I decide whether this will be a print book, an eBook, or both. Why is this necessary? Because the formatting is different.

This booklet will explain how to format your book, adapt it for print and for eBook, and explain the similarities and differences. You will begin with a "plain Jane" format and adapt that to the different versions.

As is the case with all of the "How to For You" series, the instructions are for Microsoft Word 2007, or higher. However, a computer savvy person may be able to adapt them to other word processing software.

Dorothy May Mercer

Chapter 1 Designing Pages and Type

Paragraphs

It is always best to format your paragraphs before you begin typing. Go to the Home toolbar and pull down "Paragraph." Everything you need is here. Decide how to space and indent your paragraphs and lines. You can always change it later. For detailed instructions and recommendations please see my eBook, "*How to Better Format Your Paragraphs.*"

Page Layout

Use the "Page Layout" command to design your pages, margins, orientation, and size. It is best to choose from among the "standard" sizes. The most popular sizes for novels, in inches, are 5x8, 5.25x8, 5.5x8.5 and 6x9. More industry-standard sizes are 5.06x7.81, 6.14x9.21, 6.69x9.61, 7x10, 7.44x9.69, 7x9.25, 8x10, and 8.5x11. When choosing a size, things to consider are whether this is an adult or children's book, an illustrated book, or a series. Consider how many pages you expect to have. A rule of thumb might be this: a longer novel requires a larger size, and vice versa. It is all right to set your book size and margins now, before you begin. This will not affect your later eBook versions.

Margins

For a print book, use the "custom" margins command. Under "multiple pages" click the "mirrored" margins command. Set all the margins to .5 (point five). Set the gutter to .3 unless it is an unusually thick book (over 100,000 words) in which case you might choose .4. This will determine how close to the spine your words begin. Everyone hates to have words disappearing into the center of the book. However, bear in mind that each increase adds more pages, thus more cost, to your book. Even the tiny change of .1 on your paragraph indents will increase/decrease the total pages.

Line Spacing

Unless your book is a novella, short story, or booklet (approximately under 30,000 words) I recommend setting the sentence spacing at 1.15. This will add just enough white space between the lines for ease of reading, without adding a lot of pages. Aim for a balance of white space on your pages, to avoid an appearance of overcrowding. Also be aware that, although the program offers a few default sizes from which to choose (such as 1, 1.5 and 2) it is easy to simply type in the size you want. The same is true of paragraph spacing and indentation. You can easily type over the default sizes.

In the case of a smaller book, you may want to set the line spacing to 1.5 or 2, thus increasing the number of pages. However, at this point, you may have no idea how long your book will be. In this case, set the line spacing at 1.15 or 1.2. When the entire book is written you can change it. More on that later.

Typeface

On the Home toolbar, choose a typeface and type size for the body of your book. A good way to do this is to type a sample paragraph, highlight it and scroll through the available typefaces to see which one shows best. Copy and paste this same paragraph three or four times. Highlight the second paragraph and choose a different typeface and size for this. Do the same with the third, fourth and so on. Print out this sample page. Compare and choose the best one for your print book. Most printers can duplicate all but the weirdest typefaces. You are aiming for the best possible clarity in print, while maintaining a style in keeping with your book. For instance, an historical novel will not use a very modern looking print. I happen to like Microsoft sans serif in size 12, but that is my preference for a contemporary paper book, because it prints clearly. For an historical novel I would probably stick with Times New Roman, in size 10 or 12. (We old-timers can remember when that was the only choice.)

Any eBook conversion will use its own typeface, anyway, so, in that case, it does not matter.

Once you have made your choice, select the Home toolbar again. Highlight the paragraph of your choice. Right click on "Normal." Left click on "Update Normal to Match Selection." In the future, you will use this Normal to write most of the body of your book.

There may be occasions when you need to set off a small section. In that case you can reset the style by hand, or choose among the other styles. More on that later.

Chapter 2 Style Your Chapter Headings.

Type a sample heading and copy it three or four times. Highlight the first sample and scroll through Heading 1, Heading 2 and Heading 3 on the Home toolbar. Keep going for as long as you wish. (This is fun, right?) Move over to the "Styles" section and pull down the menu. Move your mouse up and down through these selections to see what happens and your type quickly changes from one to the other. You may decide to use the default setting for Heading1, but, if you see something you like better, click on it. Otherwise, go to the Home toolbar and select from the fonts available. Try bold, underline and italic. Once you make a choice, you may change Heading 1 to reflect that choice, using the same technique that you used to select Normal. (That is, select your sample, right click Heading 1, left click Update Heading 1 to Match Selection.) It is very important to use the same Heading 1 for all your chapter headings, not only for the sake of consistency, but for later, when and if you install an interactive Table of Contents such as the Table of Contents you see at the beginning of this book. (For more info, please see my eBook, *"How to Install an Interactive Table of Contents.)"*

If you decide to use sub-headings, you will use Heading 2 in the same fashion. Examine the Table of Contents in this book, again. Notice that I used Headings one, two and three. Neat, eh? For your convenience I placed a bookmark in the Table of Contents, so that you can travel there with one click. A click or Ctrl + click will bring you back here to Chapter 3.

Dorothy May Mercer

Chapter 3 Order of Opening Pages

You will begin your opening pages in a preordained order.

Title page (always on the first odd numbered page*)

ISBN, Copyright notice, publisher, permission and rights statement. Optional Library of Congress number. (These items can go on one or two pages, as desired.)

Optional endorsements, reviews and ads.

Optional acknowledgements

Optional dedications

Table of Contents

Introduction or Prologue, if any (odd numbered page*)

Chapter One (odd numbered page*)

Always end each opening page with a page break, not a series of enters.

*Note: In the case of a print book, placing certain important pages on odd number pages will insure that they appear on the right hand page.

Note: Your print book's opening pages should be spaced and centered so that the text is nicely balanced on the page. I usually go to View/Two Pages, so that I can look through the opening pages side by side. This will help me to space the text nicely. Use the enter command to space your text down from the top of the page, and your alignment commands (left, center, right, justified) to position text. You may also use your space bar to move text to the right.

Remember: Do not use tab to position text, as it is not allowed in the Kindle eBooks.

Hint: Depending on whether you selected to indent the first line of your paragraphs, the enter command may not place your text entirely flush with the left margin. If so your Center command will not precisely center. You can overcome this by positioning your cursor in the offending space and clicking Backspace once, before you click the Center command.

Hint: If your Enter command is not giving you the exact amount of space you desire, change the font size in that particular white space. This will change the height of your Enter.

The Reverse Arrows

Now is a good time to mention a very useful tool, the reverse or undo and redo commands. Locate the curlicue arrows in the upper left of your display. These little arrows can be useful to you in many instances, for example when you wish to reverse a previous keystroke. Each time you click on a curlicue arrow it will reverse one previous stoke or command, in the direction of the arrow.

Common Mistakes:

When designing your opening pages, always end the page with a page break, or one or two enters followed by a page break rather than using a long line of "enters" to start a new page. This is true for eBooks, as well as print books. Later we will change the size and spacing a bit for your eBook. For now, space your opening pages as if it is a print book.

Do not use "tabs" to position your titles. Instead use the Home/Paragraph/Center command, or the left, right, justified commands. Be aware that Kindle does not allow "tabs."

Dorothy May Mercer

Chapter 4 Pictures

Certain books are meant to be picture books. If so that is an entirely different kettle of fish, requiring a book of its own. (See my book *How to Create a Picture Book*). However, you, the author, may desire to enter a picture into your story by way of illustration, such as a drawing or map etc. This requires a special set of tools.

First of all, be very careful when entering pictures in color. You can use them without an extra charge in an eBook, but color print is very costly. For print, it is best to keep your interior in black, white and gray scale, while your cover is in color. More on how to do that, later.

First, click you cursor in the place where you wish to insert a picture. Go to the Insert menu and choose the type of item you wish to insert. For now, choose Picture. A new window will open up allowing you to scroll through everything stored on your computer. Click your choice. Its title will appear at the bottom of your display. Click Insert and your choice will jump into your text.

We will not go into the use of copyrighted pictures, here. The subject is long and murky. When in doubt, a web search will provide more info. Just be careful that any picture you use is one that you own, have licensed, or is in the public domain. When posting pictures of people, in many cases you should have permission, unless it is

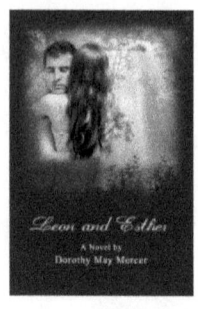 a crowd shot in a public place. For example I paid a license fee to use this picture of models.

Now, you can resize the picture and format it in several different ways. Move to the center of the picture and a four-headed arrow will appear. Click here and notice that a new choice appears in your toolbar, entitled Picture Tools/Format. Click Format and a marvelous new toolbar appears with all kinds of goodies that you can use to change your picture. One of the first things you might do is to open Size and locate the Lock Aspect Ratio Relative to original picture commands. Make sure these are checked. This will prevent you from turning the figures into skinny or fat people. Now you can resize the picture while keeping the same aspect. The easiest way to change the size is to click the picture once, and then move your cursor around the edges of the picture. Double arrows will appear. Left click and hold one of the corner arrows. Drag it in and out until you find the size picture that you want.

Next, experiment with the various commands on the Picture Tools/Format bar, until you gain an understanding of what is available.

Hint: Be aware that eBooks have a special way of handling pictures, so until you understand that, you may want to avoid pictures altogether.

Hint: You may use color in eBooks. But, a print book will charge a lot more for colored interiors, of any kind, whether it is a full color picture, or a mere footnote with one little letter in color. Here is what you do:

When formatting your color picture for a print book, open the Picture Tools/Format by clicking once in the center of your picture. Click Format. In the far left of this toolbar, in the Adjust Section, click Color. Your picture will appear in a variety of colors. Choose one of the black white and gray tone samples. Now your picture will print nicely without extra charge.

Moving Your Picture

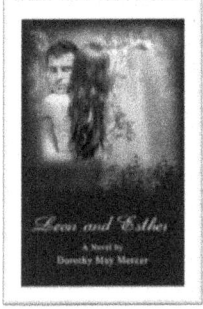

You may easily move the picture around by a maneuver called drag and drop. That is, holding a left click in the center of the picture, move your cursor to a new location and release the mouse button. You can also move it by grabbing the tiny anchor that (sometimes) appears next to the picture, drag and dropping it to the new location.

So far, your picture has taken a space between lines of text. However you can arrange your text to flow around the picture, as seen above.

Click once in the picture. Notice that grab handles appear around the edges, indicating that the picture is selected. Open the Picture Tools/Format toolbar. Go to the Arrange Section and pull down the Wrap Text menu, using the tiny arrow under the words Wrap Text. Select the way you wish to wrap your text. A good choice is Tight. Now, move your picture and text to take the most advantage of the text wrapping. You want it all to make sense, that is, don't chop words in two. Besides moving the picture, you can easily arrange the particular text, by using your space bar or your enter button. You can also highlight the text involved and justify it right, left, or center. After you are satisfied with the result, please save.

Hint: A word of caution, speaking from experience. Do not get too carried away by entering multiple pictures, shapes, and/or clip art. After all, your goal is to write a book, not a photo album, which requires a whole new set of skills.

Chapter 5 Writing Your Book

Designing Chapters

*N*ow, at last, you are ready to begin writing your book. Always start the Prologue and/or first chapter on a right hand (odd numbered) page. It may be necessary to insert a blank page to make this work. (Note: For your eBook, this rule does not apply.) Sometimes authors will start all of their new chapters on the right hand side (odd numbered page) even though it may require entering a blank page. This is nice, but not required. Whatever way you do it, be consistent.

Hint: Any blank pages that you enter will have to be removed later when you design your eBook version.

Always end your chapters with a Page Break. This is true for print and eBooks alike. You may decide to place one or two enters before your break, or before your chapter heading. However you decide to do this, remember to do it the same each time. Click the Heading command. The word Chapter and the number will often enter automatically. You can change this or add a title to it, if you choose. Click enter and the program should switch to Normal and will go to the beginning of the first paragraph. Verify that you are in Normal, now.

Styling Non Fiction

Generally, if your book is non-fiction it will proceed by chapters and sub-chapters, in much the same fashion as this book. You may even use sub-sub chapters. Notice on the Home/Styles menu there is provision for Heading 1, 2 3 and 4. Also, there is a variety of handy styles that you can use, such as "Subtle Emphasis," "Emphasis," .and "Intense Emphasis" Take a few seconds to check them out. You may use the suggestions given or create your own, as explained above.

A good way to understand this is to type a small throw-away sample, select it, and then scroll through the various options to see what happens to your sample. Unless you have a huge computer display, probably all the samples will not show. Try pulling down the menu using the arrows. You will be amazed at all that is available to you. For even more fun, pull down the Home/Change Styles menu and scroll through the dozen or so dizzying array of styles. Should you run out of ideas there is even a provision to create your own style set. Try not to spend all morning playing around with this. Remember, you are going to write a book.

Styling Fiction

Generally a chapter in your fiction book will consist of a progression of scenes. If these scenes repeat in the same location on the same day there is no problem for the reader. But, if there is a change of location, a different set of characters, and/or a skip in time, the author must use a simple device to indicate the change. After all, one cannot start a new chapter for every simple change. Not only might the result be annoying to the reader, it could result in hundreds of chapters. And so, some simple device must be chosen. I have seen lots of different choices, some quite fancy, and I admire, even envy, that. But, for myself, I prefer to make it easy, lest I waste time fooling around with doodads. Sometimes all that is needed is space. If your paragraphs are not separated by lots of space, already, simply click in one or more extra ~~carriage returns~~, (oops) enters. (Darn! I dated myself, again.) The reader will catch on quickly that extra space means a change of scene.

On another occasion, thinking I was smart and creative, I chose a fancy gizmo to mark my change of scene. After I uploaded my book to Kindle publishing, I used the review window to check the result. $%#$@^! The Kindle converter had changed all my pretty gizmos to placeholders. They would not convert. Back to the drawing board to change every single one of those fancy gizmos to something more generic.

Sometimes I use a character on my computer keyboard. Examples:

***

^^^^

^^*

~~~~~

Once you make a choice, stick with it for the remainder of that book.

I even went so far, once, to actually center the gizmo, as below: However, I soon discovered that was too much work, also I forgot half the time and had to go back and fix it, and so I simply moved my gizmo to the left and continued in that fashion for the remainder of the book. My readers do not seem to mind. It is best not to annoy the reader with too much fal-de-rall.

***

Hint: Sometimes when you type in a string of characters the Word program mistakenly thinks you want it to go all the way across the page, like this:
■■

You can fix that by clicking Backspace just once.

Alignment

Compare the following two paragraphs, not as to content, but in terms of how they look, at first glance. #1. When setting your paragraph style, you have a choice of left, center, right and justified. Personally, I like to use justified in my novels. It makes for a much neater looking page. When a potential customer browses through a bookstore display, what attracts them? Is it the cover, title, author? Perhaps it is all the above. Watch it happen, sometime. You will see the customer pick up the book, look at the cover, peruse the back cover, and finally flip through the pages. At this point, what is she looking for? My guess is that he is checking to see what the pages look like. Are they easy to read? Are they crowded or neat? Is the type clear and bright? If so, having the print justified will make it look neat and tidy.

#2. When setting your paragraph style, you have a choice of left, center, right and justified. Personally, I like to use justified in my novels. It makes for a much neater looking page. When a potential customer browses through a bookstore display, what attracts them? Is it the cover, title, author? Perhaps it is all the above. Watch it happen, sometime. You will see the customer pick up the book, look at the cover, peruse the back cover, and finally flip through the pages. At this point, what is she looking for? My guess is that he is checking to see what the pages look like. Are they easy to read? Are they crowded or neat? Is the type clear and bright? If so, having the print justified will make it look neat and tidy.

Paragraph #1 above, was left aligned, with no space between the paragraph and the preceding paragraph. The line spacing was set at "single."

Paragraph #2 was justified, with a space between paragraphs set at 10, and line spacing set at 1.15. See the difference? I think you will agree that paragraph # 2 appeared to be easier to read, even though it contained the exact same words, font and size as paragraph #1. The white space made the difference.

Chapter 6 After "The End"

Non Fiction

Footnotes

*F*ootnotes are frequently used in non-fiction, but rarely, if ever, used in books of fiction. They serve the purpose of further explanation of a word or phrase, when the author does not wish to put it in the text. Another purpose is to identify and give credit to the origin of a quote, phrase or idea. This works well if the footnote is reasonably short, but in the case of long items, it is better to use an end note. Your software will give you the choice of footnote or endnote. It will place a tiny half-raised number exactly where you place your cursor, and open up an area at the bottom of the page (or at the end of the book, as the case may be) where you type your note. In a well-constructed book, the reader can click on the number and be taken directly to the note. After reading the note, he can click back to the exact spot where he left off.

Hint: You will find the footnote and endnote commands in the References toolbar, Footnotes section. More advance commands are available in the pulldown menu, accessed by clicking the tiny arrow in the bottom right corner of the section.

Hint: When your book is converted to eBook, the server (such as Kindle) will automatically place all your footnotes at the end of each chapter.

Reference Pages

Depending on the degree of formality of your book, following the end, it is quite proper to add any or all of the following references:

    End Notes

    Credits

    Bibliography

    Author's Notes

    About the Author (with or without picture and address links.)

Note: If you are writing a formal college theme, thesis or dissertation, or a professional paper, there are strict guidelines for exactly how these references are to be written. We do not intend go into that, except to advise you, if that is your purpose, to please look for a more complete reference.

Fiction:

Typically, authors and publishers take advantage of the end space to lay in a bit of advertising. There are no strict rules for this, but it can range among these items:

    A plea for Reviews

    About the Author

Picture of Author

Author's Notes

Other books by this Author with titles, synopsis and/or where to order.

Cover Pictures of other books by this author, and/or this publisher.

Teaser peeks and chapters of the next book in the series, or others.

Almost anything goes, so long as it is lawful.

In my McBride Series, of five complex and full-length novels, I include a list of characters at the end of each book. Perhaps this is a bit unusual, but it helps the reader because there are a lot of characters in these books. I even use the reference myself.

Dorothy May Mercer

Chapter 7 Final Formatting of Print Book

Assuming your book is completed, edited and proofread, multiple times, and you have saved a Plain Jane version, you are now ready to prepare it for printing. Send any previous versions to your Trash Can.

Save two more versions and label them Print Version and eBook version. Open the print version. Check your opening pages one more time to ascertain that they are properly centered on the page. Click Save.

Creating Sections

In order to complete the following instructions please ascertain that the "show paragraph enter sign" is toggled on. I cannot draw one here, but it looks like a P backwards. When the sign is "on" you will see one of those backwards P's every time you push the enter key. The sign is located on the "Home" toolbar.

Move to the very end of your opening pages (just before your first chapter or intro.) and position your cursor just ahead of the "page break." Delete this "page break," temporarily.

Leaving cursor in place, open "Page Layout."

Click the tiny arrow next to "Breaks" and pull down the menu.

Under "Section Breaks" select "Next Page, (Insert a section break and start the new section on the next page)." This will re-enter the page break and add a section break as well. You have now divided your book into two sections for the purpose of entering different page numbers and headings in the second section.

Remember how you created two sections, because the time may come, after you have finished your book when you may wish to create a third section at the end, affording yourself the ability to have different headers in your advertising pages, especially if they contain a sneak peek of a few chapter of your next book. Don't worry about that now. Just remember where you found these instructions.

Creating Headers

Move your cursor into the first page of section 2 and click in the empty heading space, at the very top of the page.

Hopefully, the heading space will open up and the main body will be darkened. Everything you write here will show on every page in section two. In a moment we will write in this space. But first, if a header space did not open up, we need to find the Header and Footer Toolbar, as follows:

Click "View" and make sure you are in the "Print Layout" view. If not, click on it.

Now move back to "Insert" and click on it. Look for a section marked Header & Footer. You should see three choices, Header, Footer and Page number. We will be using these three, eventually. Click on "Header." A new list will open. Click on "Type text" and watch what happens. A new toolbar will open called "Header and Footer Tools/Design."

Click "Design"

In case you are lost, let me repeat this sequence for you in one place:
View
Print layout
View
One Page
Insert
Header
Type text
Design

In the Header & Footer Design Toolbar you should see a "Navigation" section and an "Option" section. Your cursor should now be located in the header section of your page. Notice that this place is identified as 'Odd Page Header Section 2' and "Same as Previous" We are going to get rid of the "Same as Previous" label notation, as follows:

In the Navigation section, click once on the words "Link to Previous." This should delete that link and the "Same as Previous" words will disappear. In a moment we will do the same thing for the even pages in section 2, but first...

In the Option section of the Header & Footer Design toolbar, confirm that you have a check mark in all three of the choices:

√ Different First Page

√ Different Odd Even Pages

√ Show Document Text

Good! Almost there!

Now click the down arrow twice to take you to the header of page two, which will show "Even Page Header, Section 2" and "Same as Previous." You will delete the "Same as Previous" words in the same way you did it for the odd pages, i.e. Click "Link to Previous" in the Header & Footer/Design toolbar in order to toggle that link to off position.

One more thing: while you are in this toolbar, notice the Position section, containing the settings "Header from Top" and "Footer from Bottom." Set each of these to 0.3 (zero point three). This will position your headers and footers within their respective section, .3 (three line spaces) away from the edge of the page. If you do not do this your printer may cut off your wording in these sections. Remember when we set the margins at .5? Good. Now all your headers and footers will be alike.

Now, you are ready to design your headers.

Designing Your Headers

Place your cursor in the header space for page two or any one of the even numbered pages. Any even page will do. (Change one and you change them all.)

In this header, type the heading for your even pages. Remember, even pages will be on the left when you open your book. On this page you will put the name of your book, and any other item you wish to add, such as a sub-title. You can position this right, left, center or justified using the justification commands and the space bar. Do not use tabs. Also, remember the tip about centering, i.e. make sure your text is flush with the left (using backspace if necessary) before you hit center. While you are designing this text, feel free to use font, size, bold, italic and underline, as seems good to you. Some folks even have a logo that they put here. Remember this will show at the top of every even page, so keep it small and informative.

You will *NOT* put a header on page one of your book, as this is a place to be fancy, and do something different, if desired.

Next, move your cursor into the header of page three and design the odd page heading. This is the place to put the author's name. Again, design it as desired.

Now, reading across left to right, the reader will see your book's name followed by the author's name. Good. This will remain the same throughout all the pages of the second section of your book, unless, someday later, you create a third section.

Installing Page Numbers

Now you are ready to install page numbers. Your cursor should be anywhere in section two. These commands are found at Home/Insert in the Header & Footer section. Choose bottom of page and select from the options available on the pulldown menu. Later you may choose

"Format Page Numbers" from the same menu. Open that command and select "Start at" and enter the number 1. You do not want it to "continue from previous section," because we are going to do something different in the previous section, which was section one, remember?

Earlier when you were designing the headers, you selected "different odd and even pages." Because of that you may need to go to an odd page and insert page numbers, the same as you did on the even page. Just make sure that you are in section 2 (not 1) and that you format the numbers the same way that you did on the even page.

SAVE.

Flip through a few pages to make certain that everything is correct, including your headers and page numbers.

Next you are ready to format headers and footers for section one, i.e. your beginning pages. It is customary to leave the headers blank, but it is your decision as to whether or not you wish to have page numbers in the footers of the beginning pages. Sometimes they are omitted. But, you can install them the same way you did in the main body of your work.

My practice is to install page numbers here, using Roman Numerals (i. ii, iii iv, etc.) But, it takes extra time, so use your judgment.

TIP: If you find something is already written in the headers and footers of the opening pages, it means that you have made a mistake. You must return to the instructions for turning off "Same as Previous" at the beginning of Section 2, and make sure the "Link to

Previous" button is turned off at the beginning of that section. Then you can got back to the headers of Section One and erase (delete) them.

TIP: If that doesn't work, you probably made a mistake in the instruction as to setting Section Break markers, found in the "Final Formatting Your Print Book" chapter 7, page 32.

Sorry, but you will need to go back and repeat. Do not despair. Remember, practice makes perfect and this is a complex learning experience. Do not expect to do it correctly the first time. Believe me, I still goof up. But, it becomes easier each time.

Did you install a Table of Contents? If so, you will need to update your table and make sure it is correct. For detailed help see my How to For You booklet, *"How to Install an Interactive Table of Contents."*

Note: Savvy computer geeks will find everything you need under Home/ References/ Table of Contents/ Update Table.

SAVE.

Remove All Color

One last thing to check: You must make sure that the interior of your Print book has no color. First, check any pictures and make sure they are in gray scale. If not follow the previous instructions found in Chapter Four Pictures, page 11.

Next, go to Home/Select and click Select All. Return to Home/Font and open the Font Color menu. Select Black. Click anywhere in a margin to turn off Select All.

Save a PDF Version

Now, you are ready to SAVE AS a PDF. Go to "File," Click "Save As." At the bottom of the next window locate "Save as Type." Pull down that menu and select PDF. Make sure the title is the way you want it. Click Save.

Now you should have four versions of your book in your special folder, as follows"

- My Book. Plain Jane
- My Book. eBook
- My Book. Print
- My Book Print PDF

Close all versions you have open and open your eBook version. You are now ready to prepare your eBook verson.

Take a break.

Chapter 8 Format Your eBook

*B*reak's over. Wake up your computer and get set to work on the eBook version. Now that you are a pro, this will be easy-peezy.

You now have a Plain Jane version that has been saved as eBook. There should be no headings and no page numbers. However, color is perfectly all right. Color pictures, color fonts–no problem. Also, please leave in the page breaks that you inserted earlier, that is, one at the end of each beginning page, and one at the end of each chapter. This will not cause readers any problem, but will make certain that important things begin at the top of a page.

The only changes that are necessary are to remove excess blank lines and blank pages. Simply go in and remove them. A few blank lines are fine, but no more than two in a row. That is all. See? I keep my promises, *most times*.

SAVE

Ads and Links

Now, think about whether there is anything you would put in an eBook that you would not have in a print book. For example, you may put links after the end. These could be links to sales pages, other books, blogs, web pages, and so on. More than likely your readers will be reading this in digital form and will be hooked up to the internet. Therefore, you can insert links to various sites where you will invite your readers to explore. If you are unsure how to do this, see my "How To For You" booklet, "How to Install a Link in Your Document."

SAVE

You now have an eBook version which can be the basis for any eBook you wish to publish, such as Kindle, Smashwords, Nook etc. Each one has its own special instructions for preparation. Generally, Kindle will accept your doc or docx document, as is. However, if you have trouble with that my "How To For You" series has a book of detailed instructions entitled, "How To Prepare Your Book For Kindle."

At this time you may want to have a PDF version of your eBook for your own use. Simply follow the previous instructions for creating a PDF, taking care to label this version properly.

Thank You !

The Complete *How to For You* Series:

By Dorothy May Mercer

How to Write Sentences and Paragraphs *in Your Novel*
How to Design & Format Your Paragraphs
How to Write Great Dialog, *Your Book Needs This*
How to Write Fiction
How to Fix Errors in Your Document, *Find and Replace Easily*
How to Format Your Book, *for Publishing*

How to Add an Interactive Table of Contents
How to Install a Link in Your Document

How to Register ISBNs and Copyrights
How to Edit a Book, *With a Friend*

Hot to Prepare Your Book for Kindle
How to Design a Kindle eBook Cover
How to Install Your Kindle Cover on CreateSpace, *and Vice Versa*
> *(Note: as of this writing, CreateSpace is in the process of selling out to Amazon. When that is over, we will delete this book.)*

How to Sell Your eBook Using Amazon Free Days
How to Use Your Books for Free Ads
How to Market Your Book, Marketing 101
How to Create a Picture Book
How to Self-Publish
How to Get an Audible Version of Your Book

For prices and ordering information please go to one of these web sites:

www.MercerPublications.com

www.Amazon.com/DorothyMayMercer

More Entertaining Books from Mercer Publications, Inc.
In business since 1993
by Dorothy May Mercer and other distinguished authors:

McBride novels available—eBook, Print, Audible, English and Spanish formats.

Starring Det. Lt. Mike McBride

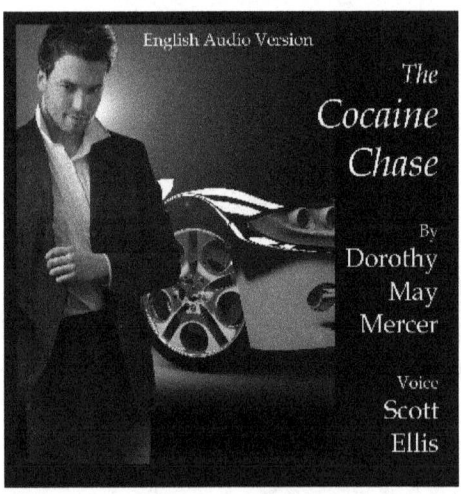

The McBride Series:

- "Car oo6 Responding"
- "The Cocaine Chase"
- "The Golden Coin"
- "The Cartel Wars"
- "The Gang Bust"

Same as above in Spanish

"Unidad oo6 Respondiendo"
"La Casa di la Cocaina"
"El Immigrant e la Monada Dorada"
"La Guerras Cartel"
"La Pandilla Busto"
The Washington McBride Series
Starring Senator Mike McBride, available in eBook, Print and Audible versions.

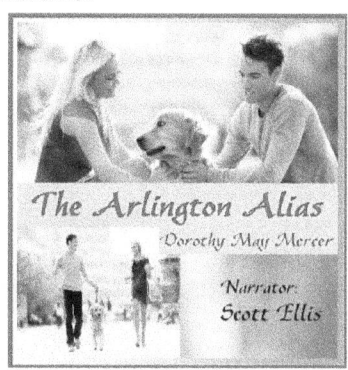

- "The Arlington Alias"
- "The Fairfax Fix"
- "The Savage Surrogate"

Starring wife Juliette McBride, investigative reporter and Lady Dog, famous Seal-trained tracking and service dog.

The New McBride Suspense (with Romance) Series

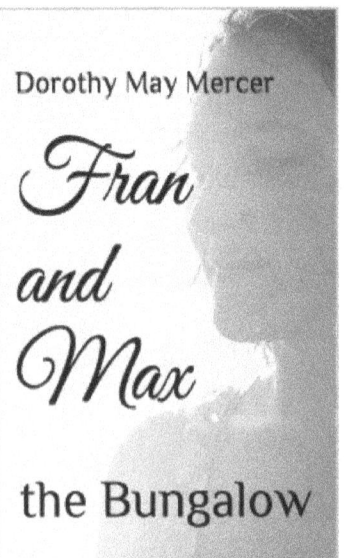

Fran and Max, *the Bungalow*
Mary Beth and Sammy, *Rolling Thunder*
Cynthia and Dan, *Cyber War*

Nate, *The Search*

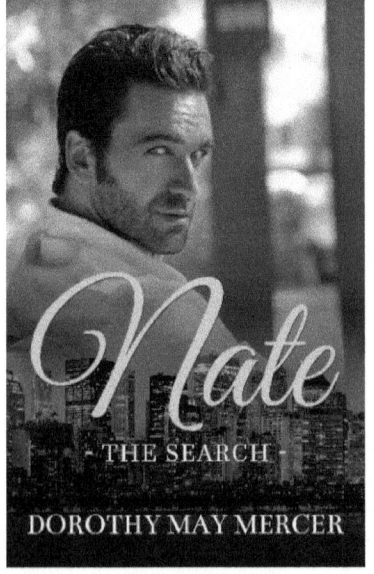

E-M-P Honeymoon, *Kelly & Tom*

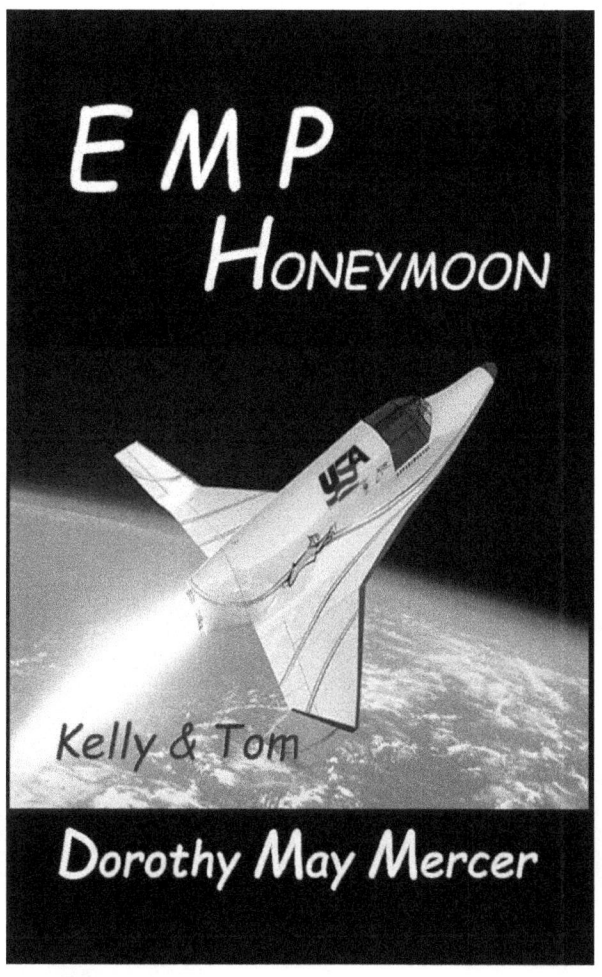

GO HERE TO ORDER THIS AND PREVIEW OTHER EXCITING AND ENTERTAINING NOVELS:

- http://www.MercerPublications.com

Historical books by Dorothy May Mercer:

- "Leon and Esther," an historical Christian love story.
- "Stories I Haven't Told," an autobiography

Travel Books With Colored Photographs:
By Dorothy May Mercer and Photographer Dave Mercer

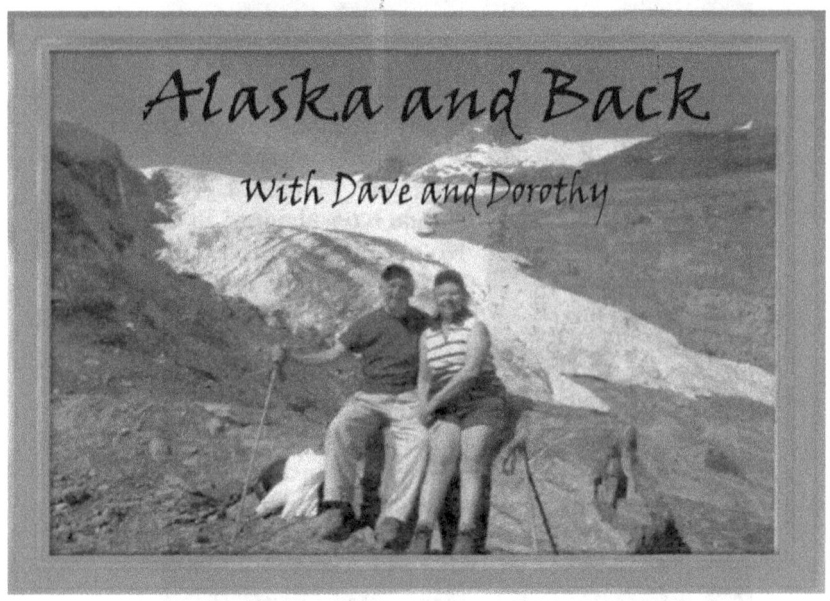

"Alaska and Back" With Dave and Dorothy, a travel journal.

"Africa and Back" With Dave and Dorothy, a travel journal with color photographs.

"Hawaii and Back" Vol. 1 Kauai, With Dave and Dorothy

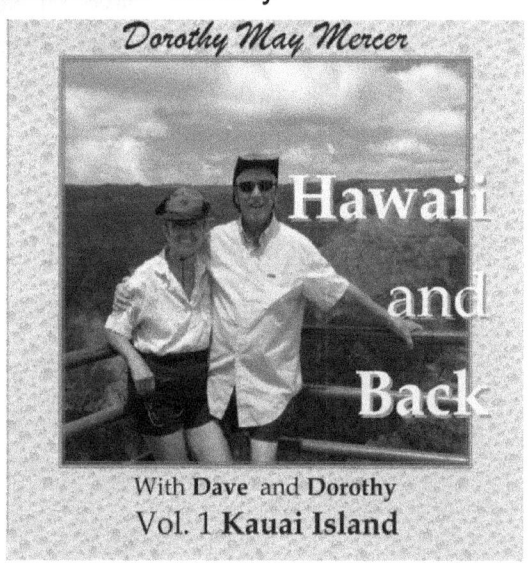

"Hawaii and Back" Vol. 2 Maui, With Dave and Dorothy

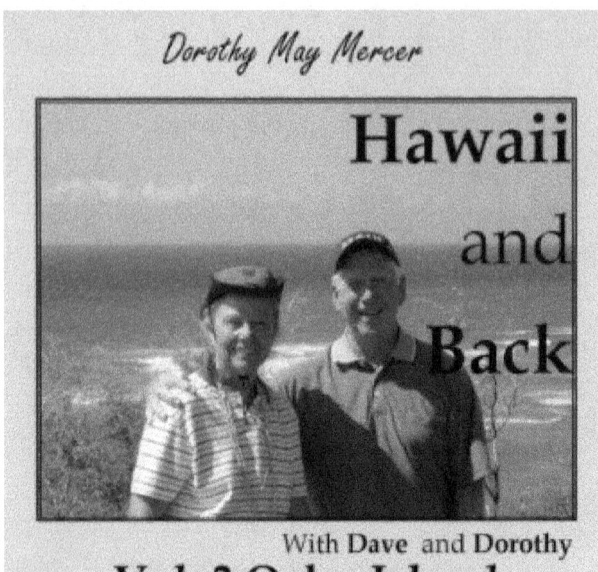

"Hawaii and Back" Vol. 3 Oahu, With Dave and Dorothy

"Hawaii and Back Via S'Fo" Vol. 4 With Dave and Dorothy

Niagara and Back" With Dave and Dorothy

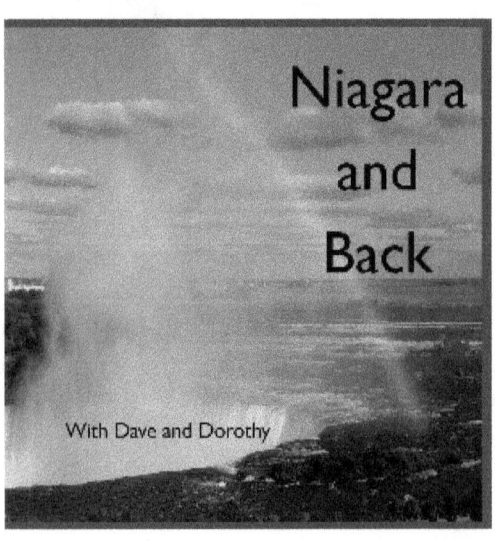

More Books edited and published by Mercer Publications & Ministries, Inc.:

~Recommended~

- "He Called Her Hat," That Tough Little Lady, by Myron C. McDonald
- "Notes from John," by Marcia McMahon
- "Ascension Teachings with Archangel Michael," by Marcia McMahon
- "Let's Talk" a Black & White Dialog in the US and UK
- "Short & Fun Stories" Vol 1 and Vol 2, by Various Authors
- "Without from Within," by Ron Shaw
- "The Yellow Bus Boys," by Ron Shaw
- "Remember How Much I Love You," by Dale L. Williams, M.D.
- "The Inheritance From Hell," by R.D. Margot
- "Stormy Affair" by Netty Ejike
- "Obsession" by Netty Ejike
- "Sensual Bond" by Netty Ejike
- "Gems" by Nancy Calumet
- Short & Fun Stories, Vol 1 & Vol. 2 by Many Friends

www.ingramcontent.com/pod-product-compliance
Lightning Source LLC
Chambersburg PA
CBHW061301040426
42444CB00010B/2468